YOUR KNOWLEDGE HAS VALUE

- We will publish your bachelor's and master's thesis, essays and papers

- Your own eBook and book - sold worldwide in all relevant shops

- Earn money with each sale

Upload your text at www.GRIN.com and publish for free

Bibliographic information published by the German National Library:

The German National Library lists this publication in the National Bibliography; detailed bibliographic data are available on the Internet at http://dnb.dnb.de .

This book is copyright material and must not be copied, reproduced, transferred, distributed, leased, licensed or publicly performed or used in any way except as specifically permitted in writing by the publishers, as allowed under the terms and conditions under which it was purchased or as strictly permitted by applicable copyright law. Any unauthorized distribution or use of this text may be a direct infringement of the author s and publisher s rights and those responsible may be liable in law accordingly.

Imprint:

Copyright © 2015 GRIN Verlag, Open Publishing GmbH
Print and binding: Books on Demand GmbH, Norderstedt Germany
ISBN: 978-3-668-05538-4

This book at GRIN:

http://www.grin.com/en/e-book/306294/a-handbook-for-small-scale-egg-production

Pedzisai Matimbe

A Handbook for Small Scale Egg Production

GRIN Publishing

GRIN - Your knowledge has value

Since its foundation in 1998, GRIN has specialized in publishing academic texts by students, college teachers and other academics as e-book and printed book. The website www.grin.com is an ideal platform for presenting term papers, final papers, scientific essays, dissertations and specialist books.

Visit us on the internet:

http://www.grin.com/

http://www.facebook.com/grincom

http://www.twitter.com/grin_com

SMALL SCALE EGG PRODUCTION HANDBOOK

PEDZISAI MATIMBE

Agriculture Teacher - Nyamande Secondary School, Zimbabwe
BSc Hons Degree in Agricultural Economics and Management – Bindura University of Science Education

PREFACE

This handbook provides useful information on how to keep layer hens profitably. It sheds light on factors to consider when selecting layer breeds, brooding and all critical management practices from day old up to marketing of eggs. Farmers need to grasp this hand book so that they will be able to produce a healthy flock. I recommend farmers to make use of this book without reservations because information and experience offered in this book is valuable. Farmers and inspired readers can make use of this hand book as a foundation to carry out researches as well as generating new ideas.

Wish you the best of all luck in egg production.

Table of Contents

- LAYER BREEDS ... 4
  - Factors to consider when choosing a breed ... 4
- BROODING ... 4
  - HOUSING REQUIREMENTS ... 4
  - Brooder hygiene ... 5
- REARING PULLETS ... 5
  - Housing requirements ... 5
  - Deep litter system ... 6
- NUTRITIONAL REQUIREMENTS ... 7
- WATER REQUIREMENTS ... 8
  - Ration changes ... 9
  - Midnight feedings ... 10
  - Light stimulation ... 10
  - Lighting programs To achieve good early Egg size ... 11
- MANAGEMENT OF POINT OF LAY HENS ... 12
  - HOUSING AND EQUIPMENT FOR P.O.L HENS ... 12
  - Floor space ... 13
  - EQUIPMENT FOR 200 BIRDS ... 13
  - Laying nests ... 13
  - Feeders ... 13
  - Waterers ... 14
  - Perches ... 15
  - House climate ... 15
  - Lighting ... 15
  - Feeding ... 15
- EGG COLLECTION AND PACKAGING ... 16
- STORAGE OF EGGS DURING THE LAYING SEASON ... 17
- MARKETING OF EGGS ... 17
  - Direct Marketing ... 17
- POULTRY DISEASES ... 18
  - VIRAL DISEASES ... 19
  - BACTERIAL DISEASES ... 20
  - INFECTIOUS RESPIRATORY DISEASE ... 21
  - PARASITIC DISEASES ... 22
  - NEOPLASTIC DISEASES ... 22

LAYER BREEDS

1. Leghorn
2. Ancorna
3. Mincorna

Most of the commercial breeds that are on the market were probably hybrids from the aforementioned breeds for example black crest and harvest.

Factors to consider when choosing a breed

1. Number of eggs laid for the whole production period.
2. Peak production age.
3. Body weight at the end of the laying period.
4. Quality of meet at the end of production period

Comperative analysis of the viability of black crest and harvest basing on the aforesaid selection criterion

Black crest	Harvest
Potential to lay 280 eggs in its life.	Potential to lay 260 eggs in its life.
Reach peak production at 32 weeks.	Reach peak production at 30 weeks of age.
Body weight at the end of laying period is 2.55 kg	Body weght at the end of laying period is 2,30 kg

BROODING

Brooding is the care given to young chickens from day old up to the forth week. Successful brooding needs the best care and the most attention since it is the pre-requisite to expeditious growth rate and handsome profit.

Housing requirements

A good brooder house must protect the birds against all sorts of external shocks such as adverse climate conditions and predators. Tight and well programmed bio-security measures are very imperative

On the first day of arrival the recommended temperature of the brooder house ranges from 33^0C to 35^0C. The temperature is relatively high because the small body mass of chicks cannot generate heat to cope with high rate of heat loss through their relatively big body surface area. Temperatures should be reduced gradually but not below 23^{0}C by the end of the 4th week down to the level of ambient temperature. The brooder house should be far away from other chickens because other chicks can pass diseases to young chicks.

The brooder house must be well ventilated to discourage the development of a humid micro-climate condition which promotes development and speedy spread of diseases. To catalyze biochemical reactions, ample water must be provided all the times to the chicks. Chicks must have a free access to correct and optimum food in order to grow fast as well as producing eggs at the right age.

Brooder hygiene

Cleanliness is the most important and integral part of brooder management programme because it affects growth of chicks as well as profits. To maximize profits farmers are recommended to formulate an exceptional hygiene programme. The surroundings of the brooder must be clean to avoid spread of diseases. Make sure you avoid damp conditions to discourage built up of coccidiosis. Always keep water and feed troughs clean to avoid contamination of water and feeds. Culling and isolating ill-health birds also avoid spread of diseases. Provision of space is also imperative because sufficient space enable chicks to move freely and enhance circulation of air.

As a general guide, about 30 – 40 chicks/m^2 can be stocked up to the age of 2 weeks. The stocking density can be lowered to 10 -15 chicks/m^2 between 2 – 3 weeks.

REARING PULLETS

Rearing of layers require more time and relatively huge capital injection so farmers are advised to practice infallible management from day 1 up to the end of production period.

Strategic feed management is important in layer chicks production. They need optimum feed for high productivity. Correct feeding stimulates genetic potential of the breed. Each layer requires 120g of feed each day and this reduce incidence of overweight. If layers become overweight they will not be able to lay many eggs.

Housing requirements

To make egg production enterprise fruitful, farmers must ensure that poultry houses are clean, comfortable and healthy. Stresslessness make layer type chick to produce well later.

Poultry keepers must be aware of the standard space for pullets up to 18 weeks old as a way of keeping them under stressless environment. At least 1 square metre of floor space is needed for five pullets.

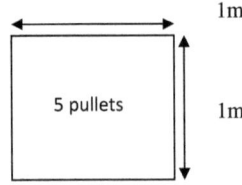

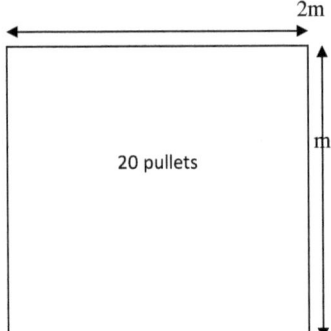

Feeding and watering space should be 100mm and 25 mm per bird respectively.

A standard housing for pullets must have the following features:

1. A solid and strong wall up to height of 1m to protect birds from external factors like predators or strong winds.
2. A wire mash for the remaining 100cm to allow sufficient ventilation.
3. An impenetrable and impermeable roof to protect the birds from predators and water leakage during rainy season.

Deep litter system

Deep litter system is the most appropriate housing system for small scale or backyard egg production. It is cost effective because it can be used from brooding up to the end of production period. Floor requirements should change with the age of the birds. Litter should be 200mm deep and is usually removed and replaced at an interval of 17 to 21 days to reduce dampness and smells spread of various poultry diseases.

Advantages of deep litter system

1. The mixture of litter and birds excrement provides valuable manure for plants.
2. The system save space as it requires a small area as compared to battery cage system.

3. Birds have room to move freely in the run. The movements burn fates and improve productivity.
4. High stocking is possible. Light can be easily provided and this enables birds to feed at night.

NUTRITIONAL REQUIREMENTS

Good feed management is essential when producing layer birds since it is the pre-requisite to production of strong and productive pullets. Day old chicks eat chick starter mash up to eight weeks. From nine to eighteen weeks pullets eat growers mash or pellets. From week eighteen layer hens eat layers mash. The table below shows types of feed and their fat and protein composition.

Table 1: nutrient requirements

Age of bird	Ration	Fat %	Protein %
0 – 8 weeks	Chick mash	5	19 - 20
8 – 18 weeks	Growers mash	5	15 - 25
From week 19	layers	4.5	16 - 20

Farmers can also use concentrates to feed layer birds. The mixing ratio for concentrates and maize is stated below:

- 2 parts chick mash concentrate to 3 parts maize meal.
- 1 part growers mash concentrate to 1 part maize meal.
- 2 parts layers mash concentrate to 3 parts maize meal.

The amount of feed required by layer chicks increase with the increase in age. The table below shows the feed requirements for 200 layer type chicks, pullets and hens.

Table 2: feed consumption for the whole production cycle (200 birds)

Age in weeks	Feed type	Feed required for 200 birds in kg/week
5	Chick mash	56
6		62
7	(chicks)	77
8		76
9		84
10	Growers mash	88
11		104
12	(pullets)	116
13		116
14		120
15		120
16		126
18		128
19	Layers mash (layers)	130
20 and above		132

In a nutshell, each layer hen requires about 120g per day.

The quantity of feed in the aforementioned table is adequate for high productivity. It allows farmers to exploit full genetic potential of the breed.

WATER REQUIREMENTS

Water is the most readily available essential ingredient of all poultry feeds. The table below shows the amount of water required by birds in different age groups.

Table 3: quantity of water required by birds daily (200 birds)

Age of birds in weeks	Approximate amount of water required for 200 birds in litres per day
5	18
6	20
7	24
8	26
9	28
10	30
11	32
12	34
13	36
14	38
15	40
16	42
17	44
18	46
19 and above	48 - 50

Ration changes

Feed rations can be changed in terms of duration not feed concentration. Do not move to the next ration until the pullets have attained breeder target weight for the appropriate age. Starter rations maybe extended until 8 or 9 weeks and grower's rations maybe fed until they goes on to pre-lay. This is especially true during high heat and depressed consumption. During periods of flock handling for bacterin infections, increase the density of the feed for some days to offset the reduction in intake. This can be accomplished by simply going from a grower's ration to a starter ration for a week to compensate for the anticipated nutrient intake reduction.

Approximate weight for the appropriate age

Age of chicks and pullets in weeks	Average mass of a chick or pullet (g)
5	370
6	435
7	510
8	610
9	700
10	750
11	900
12	1000
13	
14	
15	
16	1150
17	
18	1250
19	
20	

Accurate weekly body weight monitoring is essential to make sure that your rearing program is on track. Pullets grow speedily during their first 6 or 7 weeks of age depending with the breed, requiring high levels of protein and energy. Pullets at or above target body weight are usually the best performers during the laying period.

Midnight feedings

Midnight feedings should be utilized during heat stress periods to increase feed consumption and growth rate. Allow three hours of darkness before and three hours of darkness after the hour of light. During this one hour of light, feeders should run assuring even feed distribution to all pullets and allowing for adequate water consumption before lights out.

Light stimulation

Artificial light sources used in rearing facilities for pullets and laying houses include incandescent lamps, tabular fluorescent lamps and energy saving lamps. In order to prevent stress-induced behavioral abnormalities the light intensity in light-proof pullet and layer housing is restricted for commercial reasons to about 5 lux (rearing) and about 10-15 lux when the hens reach for weeks of age. Fluorescent tubes and energy saving lamps operating in the low frequency range (50Hz alternating current) are not suitable for fowl. Because of their sharp vision, hens perceive the flicker of the light, which can have adverse effects on their behavior such as nervousness, feather pecking and cannibalism. Preference should therefore be given to 40 watt electric lights.

Lighting programs to achieve good early Egg size

Pullets must have the standard body weight before or at the onset of egg production. Larger early egg weight is after the result of birds being heavier at sexual maturity. If the standard weight is not present at 18 weeks of age, the light stimulation should be delayed until the standard body weight is attained. [Once the flock attains standard body weight, light stimulation must be introduced so as to stimulate sexual maturity.]

Sexual maturity can be delayed by employing a lighting program that reduces the amount of light given to the pullet flock during the growing period after nine weeks. This program is called step down program. An example of a step down program designed to delay sexual maturity is shown below.

Step down program option 1

Age	Hours of light
1-2 day	24
2-7 days	18
2 weeks	17
3-10 weeks	15
11 weeks	14.5
12 weeks	14
13 weeks	13.5
14 weeks	13
15 weeks	12.5
16 weeks	12
17 weeks	12
18 weeks	12
19 weeks	13
20 weeks	13.5
21-30 weeks	15 min per week up to 17 hours

Step down program 2

Age	Hours of light
1-2 day	24
2-7 days	18
2 weeks	17
3 weeks	16
4 weeks	15
5 weeks	14.5
6 weeks	14
7 weeks	13.5
8 weeks	13
9 weeks	12.5
10-17 weeks	12
18 weeks	12
19 weeks	13
20 weeks	13.5
21-30 weeks	15 min per week up to 17 hours

This program has no effect on sexual maturity because the step down in the amount of light is stopped after 10 weeks, which is the best time when pullets become sensitive to light. This program promotes better growth in pullets by allowing more feed consumption due to additional light for the young pullets.

MANAGEMENT OF POINT OF LAY HENS

At 18 weeks old a pullet is now called a point of lay (P.O.L) hen. Purchasing started pullets, birds are 18-22 weeks of age and are ready to lay, is usually the easiest and most economical method. It is best to bring laying hens into production around 20 weeks of age. Purchasing point of lay hen avoid risks of brooding and rearing. It also shortens the payback period. If properly managed, a (P.O.L) hen should lay up to 285 eggs in the next 52 weeks.

Housing and equipment for P.O.L hens

A very good and economic place to keep layers is a well designed deep litter poultry house. Deep litter housing systems for P.O.L hens vary in design and layout depending on flock size and the type of building. The litter should be 3 to 6 inches deep and dry. Pine shavings provide best litter but any absorbent material with minimal dust is appropriate. The litter provides comfort and prevents leg problems.

Floor space

Stocking densities should not exceed three hens per m^2 of usable floor i.e approximately 66-70m^2 of space. Any less space can result in restricted feed and water consumption for some birds hence low egg production rate.

Equipment for 200 birds

ITERM	NUMBER
Nest boxes	40
Feeders	5
Waterers	6
Perches	2m long by 20

Laying nests

Laying nests should be easily accessible to the hens, preferably located along the walls or in a central position of the poultry house. It is recommended to keep the entrance to the nest well lit whereas the interior should be darkened.

Pullets should not be allowed to access to the nests too early as this reduce the attractiveness and acceptance of the nests during the laying period. The nests must be closed at night to prevent roosting and soiling overnight. It also makes nests less attractive to mites.

Feeders

Use of feeders avoids feed wastage as compared to scattering feed on the ground. There are two main types of feeders that can be used in poultry production. The types of feeders are long feeder and round feeder. Layers require at least 12cm of space along one side of long feeder dish and five cm when feeding from round feeder.

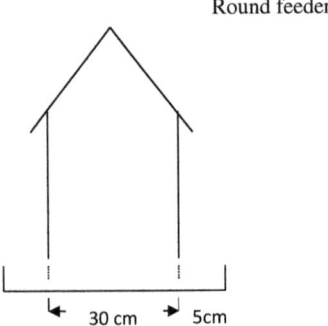

Round feeder

Ways to reduce feed wastage

1. Fill the feed trough not more than 1/3 full
2. Build lips around the edges of the feeders to catch split feed
3. Place a rotating stick above long feeders to prevent the birds from sitting in the feed and dirtying the feed.

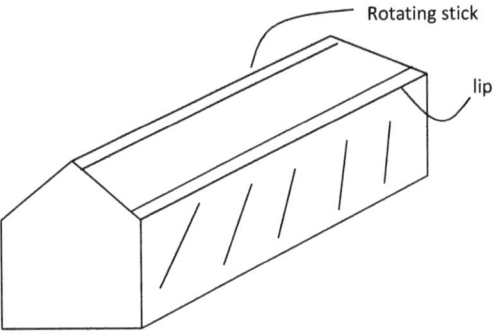

Waterers

Layers require clear, cool and fresh water. Water can be provided through the use of drinkers or waterers with enough drinking space. There are two types of drinkers that is, long drinkers and round drinkers. Drinking space with long drinkers is 2cm and 1cm space with round drinkers. Drinkers must be placed at different places in the poultry house but should not be further apart than 4 to 5m.

Perches

Perches are thin, narrow strips 5cm wide and 35 cm long, usually made of wood. Perches can be placed about 5 – 7 cm apart. Each layer hen needs approximately 15 cm of sitting place. Perches are very important because chicken like to spend the night on them.

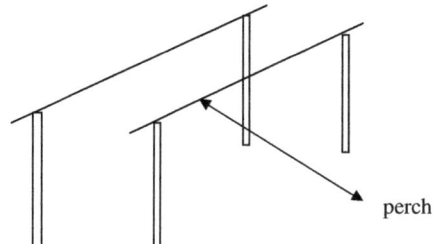
perch

In deep litter system perches need to be placed above a dropping board to keep litter warm and smart for long time. It becomes easy to collect droppings.

House climate

The optimum temperature for laying hens is 18^0C with a relative humidity of 50 – 75%. High temperatures usually above 30^0C cause heat stress therefore reduction in number of eggs layed per day. Water can be used to regulate temperatures by spraying laying hens or roof. Thatch is the most appropriate roofing material in areas experiencing high temperatures. Very low temperatures lead to increase in feed consumption rate and reduced egg production as well. Lights can be used to increase room temperature to attain the optimum temperature.

Lighting

The best light source for laying hens is a high frequency bulb emitting light within the natural spectrum above 2000Hz. As mentioned earlier, fluorescent tubes and energy saving bulbs are not suitable as they encourage feather pecking and cannibalism. For maximum production, layers need 16 hours of light.

Feeding

At 18 weeks old layer hens are ready for a change from growers mash to layers mash. Each layer requires about 120g of feed up to week 75. In egg production enterprise cost of feed is very important as it constitutes between 70% and 80% of total costs. Farmers should avoid unnecessary feed wastage to minimize production costs.

EGG COLLECTION AND PACKAGING

The most appropriate time to collect eggs is in the morning because of the eggs are laid within 6 hours of the first light in the morning. Collection of eggs in the morning reduces number of breakages and accumulation of dirty. Since eggs are easily affected by high temperatures it is imperative to collect them frequently in very hot weather. Eggs are positioned in cartons with small end down.

Cleaning

Farmers are encouraged to clean eggs to remove stains and reduce microbial load. Cleaning also add value because customers are always after quality goods. There are various methods that can be employed to clean eggs, which are dry cleaning and wet cleaning.

Dry cleaning is usually used to clean slightly dirty eggs. It involves the use of egg brush or sand paper. Wet cleaning involves the use of warm water to remove debris and stains. Egg washing should take place with a continuous flow of water or spraying to reduce water egg contact. Soaking eggs in water for as little as 1 minute to 3 minutes can allow penetration of microbes.

Packing of eggs

Eggs are very delicate so they require good packaging to reduce shell damage. Packaging prepares eggs for storage and marketing. It protects eggs from:

- Crushing while being stored or transported
- Predators
- Micro-organisms
- Tainting or putrefaction
- Loss of moisture
- Extreme temperatures

Two types of egg packages are elucidated below:

Type 1 (Cushioning material): involves the use of clean odourless husks, chopped straw, dried hay or wheat chaff in a firm basket or crate. Stuff like material decrease the risks of shell damage.

Type 2 (filler tray)

Filler trays are commonly used for egg packaging because they enable easy handling and transportation of eggs. They are made of wood pulp moulded to accommodate the eggs or plastic. Plastic trays are economic as compared to wooden trays because can be reused and are washable. The advantages of filler trays are that they allow easy inspection of eggs without touching them and they also make egg counting easy.

Storage of eggs during laying season

For the success storage of eggs during the main laying season, the following conditions must be met.
1. The eggs placed in storage room must be clean and dry.
2. Use new, clean and odourless packing material.
3. The storage room must be well ventilated.
4. The storage room must be free from tainting materials and should be cleaned regularly.
5. The storage room must be kept at constant appropriate temperature.
6. Eggs should be stored so that they are allowed to breathe.

MARKETING OF EGGS

One of the major objectives of farmers is profit maximization. Profit is the lifeblood of business so it must be earned to ensure the survival, growth and expansion in the long run. In order to achieve this primary objective in egg production robust marketing organization is imperative. Marketing is the prerequisite to creation of customers and regular innovations. Marketing close the gap between producer and consumer.

There are two main categories of marketing channels that can be employed in quest of creation of customers. The channels are Direct and Indirect channel. However direct marketing is economic and suitable for small scale producers.

Direct Marketing

Direct marketing includes the following methods of selling:
1. Farm gate selling
2. Door to door selling
3. Producer's markets and
4. Sales to local shops.

Farm gate selling

Farmers can sell eggs from the farm but this method is effective when consumers are willing to travel to producers' premises. The effectiveness of this method also depends with the number of producers in the area. When there are more producers it means competition is stiff and it calls for promotion strategies like price reduction and transport services. The major advantage of sales from the farm is that the farmers do not incur marketing cost while obtaining market price.

Door to door sales

This method is a bit labour intensive because it requires producers to walk to the customers' premises. It is the direct opposite of farm gate selling. Door to door selling is appropriate when there is stiff competition. It enables producers to take orders directly from consumers and carry only what they are assured will be bought. Jostles of eggs in transit may cause shell damage and this reduce profits.

Producer's markets

Producers may occupy a retail outlet or a corner shop in the public to sell eggs. Feasibility and viability of this method depends on rentals and turnover so farmers must be in a position to assess its feasibility. Sales in produces' markets enable farmers to make direct contact with consumers who are not able to go to the production premises.

Sales to local retail shops

This method is a little bit complex and it requires producers with good negotiating skills. The method calls for agreement between producer and retail shop owner and management regarding supply and payment methods.

Transaction costs in this method are high as compared to aforementioned methods.

Farmers can do business with institutional consumers such as food outlets, schools and hospitals. This type of direct marketing is appropriate because institutions make payments in time and they can place orders in advance.

Indirect channel involves the use of intermediaries such as:

1. Retailers
2. Wholesalers
3. Collectors.

POUTRY DISEASES

There are different poultry diseases which can pose a grave threat to egg production. Poultry diseases erode the farmers' profit maximization objectives if not properly prevented. They are categorized according to causal agents as stated below:

1. Viral diseases
2. Bacterial diseases
3. Infectious respiratory diseases
4. Parasitic diseases

5. Neoplastic diseases

It is very important for farmers to identify the threats to their poultry and how disease agents might enter a poultry farm. It is also important to identify the cost diseases and their prevention.

VIRAL DISEASES

Disease	Cause	Signs	Treatment	Control
Blue wing disease	Chicken Anaemia virus	- Syndrome in young chicks - Adult chickens do not develop signs - Depressed birds - Pale birds - Increased mortality - Focal skin lesions	No treatment is available	Vaccinate birds with CAV vaccine
Fowl pox/Avian Diphtheria	Pox virus	- Wart line lesions on the head, comps and wattles. - Depressed birds - Poor appetite - Reduced egg production	No effective treatment	
Infectious Bursal Disease (IBD)/Gumboro Disease	Birna virus of serotype	- Listless and depressed birds - Pale birds - Huddling producing watery white diarrhea - Lower weight gains and higher feed ratios - Occur between 3-8 weeks	No treatment	Use of recombinant vecto vaccines based on HVT-vector carrying an insert of the VP2 part of the IBD virus
Brittle bone disease	Avian Enteric reovirus	- Retarded growth - Poor performance and increased food conversion ratio - Brown foamy droppings - Paleness of legs and rickets	No treatment	Employ hygienic and sanitary measures

| Viral Arithritis | Reovirus infections | - Increased mortality
- Birds are reluctant to walk
- Malpositioned feathers
- Discolored and blood tinged tendons. | No treatment | - Cleaning and disinfection between cycles
- Use reo vaccines |

BACTERIAL DISEASES

Disease	Causes	Signs	Treatment	Control
Fowl cholera	Bacterium Pasteurella multocida	- Egg production will drop 5-15% - High mortality - Birds died have bluish combs and wattles - Swollen wattles	Use antibiotics	- Hygiene management - Control rodents because they transmit pasteurella multocida - vaccinations
Fowl typhoid	Bacterium salmonella gallinarum	- poor growth and depressed appetite in young birds - ruffled feathers - pale shrunken combs - drop in egg production	- use fowl typhoid bacteria - isolate infected breeder hens.	- Vaccinate layers with S. gallinarum (9R strain)

INFECTIOUS RESPIRATORY DISEASE

Disease	Causes	Signs	Treatment	Control
Newcastle disease	Paramyxovirus (APMV-1)	- High depression and death within 3-5 days - Labored breathing with wheezing - Drop in egg production - Egg shell quality affected, it becomes thin and loose in colour	There is no specific treatment but antibiotic treatment of E. coli can reduce the losses	ND is a notifiable disease but vaccines can be used to reduce losses
Infectious coryza	Avibacterium paragallinarum	- Inflammation around the eyes - Serious discharge in the nasal passage - discharge in the nasal passage	Use antibiotics like erythromycin anf tetracydine	Vaccination with multiserotype vaccines
Infectious Bronchities(IB)	Avian Coronavirus	- Depressed chicks and reduced feed consumption - Increased water intake and water droppings - Drop in egg production and shell deformation - Sometimes flock do not peak in egg production	There is no treatment but antibiotics can be used to control secondary bacterial infections	Use inactivated vaccines at point of lay to induce long lasting systematic immunity.
Avian Influenza (AV)	orthomyxovirus	- Nasal discharge depression - Reduction in egg production		vaccination

PARASITIC DISEASES

Disease	Causes	Signs	Treatment	Control
coccidiosis	Single celled parasites of the genus Eimeria	- High mortality	- Use anticoccidial chemical - Feed medication with ionophore antibiotics	
Red mite	Blood sucking mite	- Blood loss - Anaemia - Increased feed intake - Lower egg production - Blood spots on eggs	Use insectcides	- Clean the run thoroughly after removing previous flock - Poultry house hygiene
Worms		- Anaemia - Decreased egg production - Eggs with pale yolks	Treat with anthelmintics like fenbendazole	Remove litter after each cycle

NEOPLASTIC DISEASES

Disease	Causes	Signs	Treatment	Control
Marek's disease	Alphaherpes virus	- Weight loss - paralysis	There is treatment for affected flocks	Use MD vaccines
Big liver disease	Retrovirus	- lower egg production - visceral tumours found in the liver and kidneys	There is no treatment.	

YOUR KNOWLEDGE HAS VALUE

- We will publish your bachelor's and master's thesis, essays and papers

- Your own eBook and book - sold worldwide in all relevant shops

- Earn money with each sale

Upload your text at www.GRIN.com
and publish for free